AWKWARD PEOPLE OF THE BIBLE

A 30 DAY DEVOTIONAL

BY TARA JOHNSON

I would like to say thank you
to the people who believed in me!

My husband Kevin Johnson
My Girls Madison, Klara & Phoebe
Pastor Andre & Ambra who inspire me
to reach for my forgotten dreams.

My friends
who came around and
used their gifts to make this happen

Stacy Toft
Heidi Widell
Jason Fay

My Family, those who went before me
and the generations to come!

INTRODUCTION // AWKWARD MOMENTS

Today I am thinking about what it means to be awkward. I think everyone at one time or another has felt as though they were awkward. It doesn't mean that you do not know how to interact with others. Feeling awkward means you are uncomfortable in a particular scene or situation.

I personally have a hard time reading about awkward moments, and particularly watching them happen in movies. For example: I have some friends that LOVE to watch the movie *Never Been Kissed* with Drew Barrymore. This movie makes me cringe in SO many ways! The movie is about a journalist who goes "back to school" even though she is an adult. This experience drudges up all her high school memories of being awkward. The movie is hard for me to watch, but the message I pull out of it – that I think about often – is, if we understood where we were going to be in five years, the endurance of the awkward feelings would not be so bad.

If you knew in high school where your journey would take you in the next 10 years you would be less focused on your awkward circumstances, and more focused on your destiny and dreams.

The purpose of this book is to take you from the awkward situation(s) you are in now, and help you change your focus. My desire is that you would see yourself in 10 years, and understand that the Lord is equipping through uncomfortable moments to become a success. The awkward feelings you have right now are real, but they are a tactic of the enemy. These feelings are a tool to get you off focus. They are a tool that will stop you from looking into the future and destiny that the Lord has for you; your Kingdom purpose.

We all have a Kingdom purpose. The Lord has a plan for each of us. Throughout the Bible we see the Lord choose the most unlikely person, and show through them and the situation his glory, wisdom, and power. There are countless stories that flood my mind about how the Lord showed up in our awkwardness. And out of our awkwardness He empowers us to reach our rightful destiny as sons and daughters of the Most High!

The next 29 days are going to take us through a journey of evaluating our own destiny and asking ourselves questions, as we learn about purpose and identity through the lives of some awkward people in the Bible. They will help show how to become more Kingdom focused. Tomorrow we will begin, but today I would like you to answer the following questions:

QUESTION // ANSWER

What makes you feel the awkward?

How has this feeling prevented you from doing things
you felt the Lord was/is asking you to do?

DAY 2

When one thinks about the awkward people of the Bible, Gideon is often on the tip of people's tongue.

When the Angel of the Lord appeared to Gideon, his reaction was not hard to believe. He was shocked the Lord had found favor in him. "...My clan is the weakest in Manasseh, and I am the least in my father's house." And when the Lord reassured Gideon that He would be with him, Gideon still argued, and said that he was the "least" in his own house.

Can you relate to Gideon? Maybe you have someone who really inspires you: a teacher, your parents, a youth pastor – someone who really believes you can do anything, but you feel inadequate. You cannot understand how they can have SO much faith in you! But they keep pushing you, until you step out and try.

Or, maybe you don't have anyone who is pushing you. You feel lower than low, that you are not good enough, not smart enough, not _____ enough to do whatever it is you feel like you want/desire/are supposed to do. DO NOT believe that lie! YOU are NOT alone!

God believes in you, just like He believed in Gideon. What happened to Gideon? Does he just follow the Angel of the Lord and go after what the Lord had asked him to do? NO! Gideon asked for a sign! Can you believe that!? I don't know about you, but I think I would take seeing an Angel of the Lord as a pretty big sign that God was with me. Not Gideon, how awkward is that (still doubting after all those signs)? But, in Gideon's defense, in verse 22 it says, "Now Gideon perceived that He was the Angel of the Lord…" So he didn't really recognize that it was God sending a message to him.

Maybe someone has told you the Lord was going to do something great through you, and perhaps it was hard for you to believe. Perhaps you have had dream and thought it was just a dream caused by bad pizza when it could really have been the Lord speaking prophetically to you. If we are not secure in our identity in Christ, or know His voice, and what He has called us to do; when people give encouragement they feel is from the Lord, you may write off those words, and tell yourself "they don't really know me" or "that could never be me I am too ___" (fill in the blank with whatever lie you are believing about yourself). Our security and identity need to be found in Christ. We need to learn to know Him and discover who He is calling us to be. Otherwise, we can be caught unaware like Gideon and delay the word of the Lord through our own lack of understanding or do things we were not meant to pursue.

Again, as the Lord asks Gideon to deliver the people of Israel, he asks for a sign. This is a lesson for us. Part of growing in the knowledge and understanding of who God has called you to be is to test the word of the Lord as it comes to you. Sometimes that testing means taking a leap of faith, like we see Gideon test with the fleece. NOT just once though – TWICE… just to be sure! I can totally see myself doing this? Have you ever tested the Lord like this?

You say to yourself, "Okay God, if that is really you then _____"; and then just to be sure it wasn't a fluke you ask Him to do whatever it was again. I think sometimes even this can lead us to feel awkward; when God DOES answer you and answers you again. The greatest thing that we learn from Gideon is God is so patient with us in our own doubt and uncertainty. He saw Gideon as a mighty man of valor, but Gideon didn't identify with that until he had proven the word of the Lord.

It is my opinion that the Lord didn't mind when Gideon had to test Him. God already knew the outcome. You have to remember that you are not here on this planet going through the steps you are going through, for God's benefit, or for Him to find out how great you are. God already believes in you! He is just waiting for you to believe enough in yourself to take a leap of faith in Him. To trust that He is there to catch you when you fall, and to cheer you on when you succeed!

QUESTION // ANSWER

How can you relate to Gideon? Do you feel like the weakest in any area of your life?

How has God shown you that He is there for you when you have taken a leap of faith?

If you never taken a leap of faith, or maybe you have and you feel like God is asking you to again, take a leap of faith, what is it?

How can you take your circumstances, or the way you think about yourself and re-frame your identity? Gideon saw himself as the lowest of the low and God saw Gideon as a "Mighty Man of Valor!" How can you relate?

DAY 3

HOSEA 1 // GOMER // WHAT A NAME!

We see in this part of the story that Hosea was given specific instruction on what to name his children. Each of them had a destiny as part of Israel's future. Even though you may discover that your name means something you don't like or is not something like "Peter, which means Rock", that God can link purpose to, your name is powerful and help identify your call.

So many people despise the name they are given. In these instances I think about Saul, when he had the Damascus road experience that you read about in Acts Chapter 9. Not only does he see his future and the error of his ways, God gives him a new identity.

Your name is part of your identity and God can give you a new one. Maybe you have been plagued by the "sins" of your past. Ask God to speak to your identity and change it. Dig deep into the Word of God and discover who He says you are.

Understanding who you are is the biggest part of walking in the uniqueness of how God formed you. You are the only you that there is, you cannot be replaced. You might think you're awkward, or your name is weird, but make no mistake: God has a plan and purpose for you! You were not put on this earth by accident; the Lord put you here to have relationship with Him. The enemy of our flesh comes to distort that reality and projects his own awkwardness onto us so that it keeps us separated from the unconditional love of our Heavenly Father.

QUESTION // ANSWER

Look up what your name means? Family name?
How do you think the meaning of your name relates to
the call God has placed on your life? Does it help you
identify a call that maybe you didn't realize was there
before?

How does having a clear picture of your identity help
you form your calling?

DAY 4

HOSEA 3 // GOMER // A BAD RAP

Yesterday we looked at Gomer and Hosea's children and how God gave specific names to each of them. Today I want to focus on Gomer. What an awkward name. When I was praying about who to include in this devotional, Gomer was THE first name that popped into my head. But what does Gomer's name mean? Who was Gomer? In Hebrew, Gomer's name means completion. God was so upset about Israel's unfaithfulness that He has His prophet marry a harlot so He could display His love and patience for His people through Hosea's relationship with Gomer.

The story of Gomer is a redemptive display of God's love and a foreshadowing of Christ continuing to take back His bride despite her betrayal. Throughout the story we see Gomer leave Hosea, and go to other men; and Hosea takes her back multiple times. Gomer's purpose, even her name was indicative of this, to show God's completion with Israel, and that He would always take Israel back.

Have you ever felt like because you were connected to someone who had a negative reputation that people would feel the same way about you? If you think about it, Hosea could have thought the same thing, that everything Gomer did was going to be a direct reflection on him. But Hosea knew his destiny spanned beyond his relationship with his wife. He knew the most important thing in the world was his relationship with God, and his obedience to the things the Lord asked him to do. He was not concerned with what other people thought. This should be true in our own lives.

When things don't seem like they are going our way or look like it could reflect poorly on us, we need to remember we are called to something greater. We are called to be in relationship with the Heavenly Father and He is here to be sure that we are on the right path for our identity and calling.

Christ took on all our sin. Do you think as Christians we always reflect the best representation of Christ in everything we do? Sure you may not be a harlot, maybe you are – no judgment here. Christ always takes us back. Each time we make a mistake, He is quick to forgive and forget. We are incapable of this kind of unconditional love without the grace of God in our lives. It is His love that He asks us to display, not our own. He gives us the strength out of His own to display His love.

Not only did Hosea display unconditional love for Gomer, he also understood his reputation didn't depend on his wife or the fact that her name was associated to his. Hosea knew his reputation was not dependent on the people of Israel, but was in his obedience to the task that the Father had given him.

QUESTION // ANSWER

Are there places in your life where you are holding so tightly because "your name is on it"?

How has someone shown you unconditional love? That someone could be Jesus.

Are there any areas in your life that God has asked you to display His unconditional love, but it has been a struggle?

PSALM 119:105-112 // WHY DO I FEEL AWKWARD?

Do you ever think about that question? Why do I feel awkward? What is it that makes me awkward? Often I find anyone who truly admits that they are an "awkward" person, is insecure in how God made them. The enemy comes to kill, steal, and destroy. He comes to kill your dreams, steal your identity, and destroy your destiny.

The enemy came in the beginning in the garden and stole our identity when He made Adam and Eve question their relationship with the Lord. In all things he (Satan) makes us question who we are and who the Lord made us to be. We were given dominion over the earth to rule as kings and queens, but the enemy of your flesh comes to persuade you to give up your inheritance and live on earth as he would have you live.

You were not made to have all this confusion in your identity. Christ came on the cross to restore us to right relationship with God and to sit with Him in heaven as joint-heirs with Him.

There are so many reasons that you can feel awkward about who you are, I don't even have to list them here, you are already thinking of them. I want you to think for a moment: Have you ever watched a movie where the plot was so obvious you felt like yelling at the people on the TV screen? You already knew where the storyline was going and got frustrated because it seemed to drag on? That is what the enemy's attacks on your identity are like!

The truth is, all the areas that you identify as area's you feel awkward, those areas are where the Lord is likely preparing to use you the most. Do you feel you are not a good speaker? That can be the enemy tricking you into thinking that you don't have anything to say – and the Lord wants to use your voice and words to bring freedom to other people's lives.

Perhaps you feel you are not smart in certain areas and feel awkward because you think it should be easy. What is the Lord saying to you? If you think that the Lord is up in Heaven believing that you are not good enough – you are believing a lie! The Lord is proud of you and has equipped you to discover the destiny He has for your life through the desires of your heart.

Oftentimes we start to feel awkward because we don't fit into the societal mold. Well, the Lord has not called you to fit into that mold anyways! Do not be conformed to this world but be transformed by the renewing of your mind. In Romans 12 Paul is trying to help you understand that every day you need to wash your mind with the Word of the Lord, to be transformed, and confirm your identity. We need to renew daily because the enemy hits hard after our identity. He wants to change and transform the image God desires us to have with his own distorted one.

We are going to unpack why you feel awkward, but that is going to take some prayer, and some reflection. You need to be willing to honestly look at your life and ask yourself and the Lord a few questions.

QUESTION // ANSWER

Are there any lies I am believing about God? The Father, the Son, and the Holy Spirit?

What lies do I believe about myself? And where does that lie come from? (DRAW IT BELOW)

What declarations do you need to write and read about yourself everyday?

DAY 6

I can bet that if I asked you to pick the most awkward of the disciples, Peter would be first to pop into your head. Thomas might have been second, but Peter was definitely first. Maybe you don't think any of the disciples could be awkward – I mean they walked with Jesus, they had to be the best of the best, right?

Peter would qualify for awkward by today's standards, hands down. He was a fisherman – which in today's society would roughly equate to a loud trucker. If you can think of all the stories of Peter, he totally fits that bill! I am not judging at all, I know some amazing men of God, who are also truckers, and also REALLY awkward. Being awkward is what sets them a part. Peter had to be awkward enough to fully trust in Jesus, having just have met Him, with Jesus saying follow me, and Peter, along with his brother, drop EVERYTHING and follow Jesus. We know that Peter had a family as well. He had to have a special kind of gift of faith to trust, know that his family would be taken care of, and follow Jesus to become a fisher of men.

Being awkward does not mean that you are the nerdy kid in the back with buckteeth and glasses, you may or may not be. If you are like Peter though, maybe you are so confident in yourself and your faith that when you know or trust something you follow it, regardless of how crazy it seems. Following Jesus while having his own family to support, had to be hard for Peter and for other people to understand. How do you leave everything you know and follow after someone.

Jesus didn't offer Peter anything outside of making him a fisher of men.

Is that is you? Do you relate to Peter? Are you a little outspoken or over confident in the things that you know? Has that ever put you in a situation where you are left feeling a little awkward? Peter is such a great example of having awkward feelings, but pushing though them to be obedient. Another great example is the story where Peter gets out of the boat and walks on the water toward Jesus. That had to be an awkward feeling of trust and uncertainty. We know that fear, which is the root of awkwardness, does take Peter over, and he begins to sink.

Sometimes the Lord will ask us to do things that may leave us feeling unsure because it seems opposite of what is 'normal". It makes me think of healing evangelists, like Smith Wigglesworth, who in the name of the Lord would see crazy miracles through outrages steps of faith.

The Lord may call you to step out in faith in awkward or outrageous ways in your future. Are you seeking out your identity so that you are willing to follow when He calls? Are you preparing to leave everything you understand behind and follow the leading of the Lord? Peter wasn't always perfect, and the Lord doesn't expect you to be either, He just expects you to be obedient.

QUESTION // ANSWER

Is there an area in your life that you need more
confidence?

What area's do you need the strengthen your identity?

JOHN 17:6-10 // PETER // AGAINST THE GRAIN IS ALWAYS AWKAWARD

Being in the world, but not of the world, is often a puzzling statement. How are you in something, but not a part of it? It requires a few key ingredients. The first of these is understanding who you are. This is a season in your life where if you are not sure who or whose you are, you should be pouring through the scriptures to identify who you are and what the Bible tells you about yourself and your destiny. It also requires "going against the grain".

Said another way, "coming at it from another direction" or even, "coming in the opposite spirit". All these refer to taking what is normally accepted and doing the opposite of that. One of my favorite games to play has always been opposite day. Where you go around, say and do the opposite of what is expected. This is basically what is being asked of us, as we go into the world but do not become a part of it.

Case in point. What if one of your friends comes up to you and starts talking badly about another one of your friends? The "normal" reaction might be to either listen or to join in on the conversation, but what if you did the opposite? What if you told your friend you didn't want to be a part of that conversation? What if you walked away if that friend wouldn't stop? Sure that friend might get his/her feelings hurt at first, but wouldn't you prove your friendship is worth having? That no matter what, you are not going to talk behind someone's back? This is going against the grain.

Going against the grain will not always feel rewarding or worth it, but in the end, when you look back over your lifetime, you will see the fruit of your labor. The labor of swimming upstream when all your friends are flowing with the current of life downstream.

The biggest tool you can have on your side when it comes to not being of this world is to always understand who the Lord has made you to be. Understanding your identity is so important when you are trying to remain strong in your faith. If you have not done some exploration go to your Bible, there are a few verses here that will help you begin you exploration. Begin to unpack the reality of who you are and what God has placed inside of you. You will be much better equipped to go against the grain and to follow the path the Lord has before you through understanding your identity.

QUESTION // ANSWER

Do you have your identity written out in a declaration somewhere you see every day? *[Genesis 1:27, Ephesians 2:10, Romans 8:14,15, John 15:15, Isaiah 64:8, Ephesian 1:13]*

How are you making an effort to not be of the world?

DAY 8

JOHN 18:1-11 // PETER //FEAR IS THE
ROOT OF AWKWARDNESS

Do you ever wonder why you feel awkward and afraid at the same time? It is because fear is the root of awkward, the fear of being different than what everyone else calls normal. In the Bible they don't ever use the word awkward, but you can no doubt compare your own feelings to those in the Bible. I want to talk about Peter and his awkwardness on the night leading up to Christ's crucifixion.

Peter was very outspoken. We know that he would have had an opinion about Christ's death. In fact, we know he did. He tells Jesus he is not going to let anyone harm Him or let Him die. Jesus immediately rebukes Peter, but not really him, the distraction that was grabbing hold of Peter and using him at that time. Not only that, Jesus prophesies that Peter will deny him three times before the rooster crows – awkward feeling of the night number one.

The second feeling of awkwardness would come when Jesus asks the disciples to stay up with Him praying in the garden. They all fall asleep, and again Jesus rebukes them. Wow, feeling really awkward now! The next awkward Peter moment is when they come to take Jesus. Peter begins to fight and cuts off the ear of one of the guards. Peter is three for three this night. Jesus heals the guard and tells the disciples not to worry.

Now Peter, who I am sure you can relate to, is replaying the night over and over in his mind. If he is anything like me, when I say or do something awkward I tend to beat myself up for it. Have you ever said or done something that you thought was amazing, or the right thing, or super smart – only to have someone tell you that you made a mistake. Well, lucky for Peter he gets another opportunity to overcome on this night.

When the disciples get to town people begin to recognize Peter, and out of fear he denies knowing Christ. Not once, not twice, but three times before the rooster crowed. I bet Peter felt ashamed. I bet he was in the depths of despair. What I love about this story is Peter gets to see Jesus resurrected. Christ visits them and Peter is radically moved. He is able to be redeemed from his denials and awkward moments from that night.

Have you ever done something that seemed like it would disqualify you from your future. It was so awkward or wrong, like cutting off a man's ear. If Peter can recover from his night of awkward moments and mishaps, don't you think that the Lord is gracious and will give you more chances! Because of Peter's understanding of love, Christ told him "on this rock, I will build my church". On Peter's understanding of Christ, the Christian church was born. Peter had one bad nigh, sure it was really bad, but not bad enough that he could not fulfill his purpose/future!

Don't let your mistakes, mishaps, or awkward moments prevent you from walking in the truth and the call that God has for you.

QUESTION // ANSWER

Is there a moment that you replay in your head over and over feeling bad about it? Ask the Lord to reveal Himself in the situation. (Use prayer of Forgiveness at the end of the book)

If there are areas in your life you need to as forgiveness of (repent)? Do so now, don't wait. Get right with the Lord, so that when your future presents itself you can be ready.

1 PET 2 // A HOLY PRIESTHOOD
DISPITE OUR AWKWARDNESS

We know that after Peter's denial of Christ, and that tragedy of an awkward day/night before the crucifixion of Christ, Peter went on to be a great Apostle, which means sent one. He sends a series of letters out into the Christian community admonishing them during a time when they are being persecuted for their faith. In 1 Peter 2:1-12, Peter lays out a foundation for Christians among non-believers.

This is a great place for us to look at how we are called to be Christians among non-Christians today. He says in verse 9...

"you are a chosen generation, a royal priesthood, a holy nation. His own special people, that you may proclaim the praises of Him who called you out of darkness into His marvelous light".

Did you realize that you are a chosen generation? Peter wasn't saying that the only people he was writing to were chosen. He was saying that all that proclaim the praises of Him, Christ Jesus, are a chosen generation. Yes, you are a chosen generation. He says in verse four that men will reject you.

Peter is expressing to the people of his time, (what I have been trying to express to you through this daily study) You are not of this world. In fact, you are awkward, but that awkwardness is to be admired. Your awkwardness is what sets you apart from the rest of the world. Peter reminds us to not be of the world and to "abstain from fleshly lusts which war against the soul". This journey that you have been placed on will not always be an easy one. We have said all along that there will be a battle, and Peter reminds us again that there are things you will have to reject that will WAR against you; to stop you, to kill, steal, and destroy you! Don't let it.

Peter reminds us that though we are awkward and out of place, let our conduct be honorable. Be in the world but not of it. Even though you are awkward and that may attract some attention, the more respectable you are the less ammunition the enemy will have to fire your way. People of the world will look upon you with respect as you keep the statutes (the rules and guide-lines) of the Bible.

In conclusion:

- Don't be of the world.
- Follow the rules of the world as long as the don't contradict God's rules.
- You are set apart.
- People will respect you and have no evil thing to bring against you.

QUESTION // ANSWER

How do non-Christians see you?

What is your reputation?

Are there areas that you need to repent and change?

How will you display the love of Christ for all to see?

EXODUS 3:1-4:17 // MOSES // WHO?

Moses
(Said in the Charlton Heston God voice - Moses the
movie is a really old movie, black and white, you should
watch it, really, you should)

Moses!? Who would have ever thought the deliverer of the Israelites was awkward? Okay, only one hand raised (ha-ha, just kidding). But seriously – have you read the book of Exodus? There is no doubt that Moses was actually awkward, or at least would have been considered awkward these days.

We see right away in the Biblical account of Moses that the first thing Moses does when God calls him to be the deliverer of the Israelites is to look at all the things he thinks disqualify him for the destiny God sees in him.

How often do we do that? How often do we feel God calling us, whispering to us, tugging at us to do something for Him, and we immediately start to tell God all the reasons we can't do it? It makes me laugh at myself when I start to do it. God is always faithful to remind me that He is God, and He already knows all my deficiencies. He knows my weakness, but He reminds me that in my weakness, He is made strong. When He knows I can't do something on my own, it makes a way for Him to come, be the loving Father He is and help me out.

God did this for Moses. In Exodus 3:12-13, He tells Moses It's okay, I am going to be with you. Tell the people of Israel that the God of their fathers has sent Me to you, and they will receive you. Not only did God call Moses, He prepared the hearts of the people of Israel to receive him. Have you ever thought that the Lord sent you to do something but you were to afraid of how others might react so you didn't follow through? This is a great example of how God prepares a way for all the things He asks us to do.

Part of becoming more equipped to hear the voice of the Lord and not feel so awkward when you are asked to step out, is to get into the Word of the Lord and study all the ways that He calls people. If you really understand how God speaks and how He calls people, then reaching inside the stories of the Bible helps you to see that God calls whom He chooses. He is not after the biggest, greatest, most beautiful person, He is after you!

The world is constantly sending us a message that if we don't look a certain way, or act a certain way, then we are awkward, nerdy, uncool, or whatever pop culture word is used to describe the least likely of society. The world or more accurately, the enemy, wants you so focused on yourself and your deficiencies so you can't see or begin to strive for the destiny that God has placed on your life.

Being awkward by pop culture's measurement does not mean you will be ineffective in your fulfillment of your identity. Maybe you are having a hard time relating to Moses as an awkward individual who, because of obedience, stepped out and actually impacted the Kingdom for God. Let's talk about some amazing people that you can relate to right now that are making an impact in society. What about Bill Gates? He was not the star of the football team, or the "get all the girls" guy – but he is now one of the richest people on the planet. This is just one mediocre example of what happens when you push through the awkward feelings you have, to start putting one foot in front of the other, and seek your identity and the destiny that God has on your life.

QUESTION // ANSWER

What do you think makes you stand out from the unique and/or different?

What do you see around you that you would want to change? Are your friends enslaved, or "trapped" following the world around them?

EXODUS 4 // MOSES // A PUBLIC
SPEAKING NIGHTMARE

Moses' first reaction to the Lord calling him was to point out his inadequacies. He argues and tells the Lord he is not good enough. Then the Lord tries to reassure Moses by revealing all the miraculous signs He is going to do through him; but Moses is still self-conscious about the way that he speaks.

Moses explains to God that he has a stutter and is not very bright. He asks the Lord again to send anyone but him. This upsets the Lord. What you need to know is that God's character IS the fruit of the spirit; He is patient, He is kind, He is long-suffering, etc. God is angered at Moses' distrust in His plan, but He lovingly reveals that Aaron, Moses' brother, will go and help be his spokesperson.

Have you ever felt like the Lord is calling you to do something that you are unqualified to do? Maybe your parents or your youth pastor keep talking to you about sharing Jesus with your friends? Or you have a big presentation coming up and you know the topic front and back, but you are still terrified to get up in front of anyone to give the speech? Maybe you can relate to Moses.

The point of this awkward moment is that God calls who He calls, and we may not fully understand why God calls us. We may not see ourselves as the sons and daughters of a king yet, but God has equipped you. There is a saying: "God has not called the equipped, He has equipped the called." God didn't call the best looking, most eloquent, and brightest person of the Hebrew people to lead them out of captivity. He called Moses.

Moses was placed in the temple, grew up in the palace as an Egyptian, and God called him. He had a stutter and by the time the Lord had called him he had committed murder and run away.

As Christians, we need to unveil the truth; when Christ died on the cross and ascended into heaven He was seated at the right hand of the Father and reconciled us to Him so we can share in His seat at the right hand of the Father. The Lord never intended for the Hebrews to be under the rule of pharaoh, so at the right time, when their hearts had turned back to God, He sent a deliverer. He sent a deliverer for you, too.

If you are struggling with school, with your friends or family, or if you feel out of place or that you are not equipped, remember, neither was Moses. He ran away and had a stutter – but God used him. God had a plan and destiny for Moses. When the enemy comes to disrupt your destiny, be quick to acknowledge it. Ask the Lord to help you. You will be amazed at the ways in which He will come through for you. Maybe the Lord will send you an Aaron to help you and be your spokesperson, or maybe you will be an Aaron for someone else.

QUESTION // ANSWER

What project, task, or job has God called you to now
that you don't feel equipped to complete?

What circumstances has God placed you in that are
stretching you beyond your abilities right now?

Middle school has been defined as one of the hardest and most awkward times in adolescent life. Bodies are changing, hormones are out of control, you are no longer a child and adulthood is still some way off. I say this is a lie from the enemy!

This is a defining time in your life. In Middle School, the decisions you make are laying the foundations of how those choices will define you the rest of your life. Many of us had hopes and dreams from middle school that have long since been forgotten.

What if we began Middle School by believing this was the best time of our life and this was the time that we were to press in, seek after God, and the plans He has for us, and the desires of our heart that He wants to see us fulfill? Perhaps you are at a different time in your life (already beyond Middle School), and maybe you feel like even at your age you are awkward and can-not seem to find your place. Or you even feel like you missed your chance and missed your calling.

What if we believed that our parents and teachers were actually here to guide and protect us? What if we started believing that God has a plan and purpose for our lives, no matter what stage of life we are in? So often in Middle School we are under the impression that everyone is out to get us, and that adults don't understand what we are going though. We feel misun-derstood, isolated and alone. That is the work of the enemy. The devil feels isolated and alone and he there-fore wants to put you in that same box. He projects his feelings and insecurities onto you. Maybe you are an adult and you still have that feeling of being isolated and alone. I challenge you to seek the Lord. He will give you opportunities to step out in obedience and discover that you are truly not alone.

We have looked at Gideon. He felt like he was the least of the least, God called him a mighty man of valor and delivered the Hebrew nation through him. Gomer and Hosea; a woman most people would deem unworthy was shown unconditional love, and had her heart turned toward her husband and her God, and acted as a representation of the Hebrew people during a time of rebellion. Moses was an orphan adopted out of the Hebrew culture into the house of Pharaoh. He had a stutter and didn't see himself as smart enough to serve as the deliverer of the Hebrew people. And what about outspoken Peter, he was launched as one of the Apostles.

Despite the glaring stories of awkwardness, God used them to help shape and define the times they were living in. They changed the course of history by seeing God and seeing beyond their own awkwardness. What if you could see beyond your own awkwardness? What if you could see the where it is that God is calling you to? What if you were obedient to the things that He asked of you even if they made you afraid. Lean not on your own understanding but in all things seek the Lord.

QUESTION // ANSWER

Where is God calling you?

Which of these four awkward people do you relate
with most? Why?

How are you going to reach out and grab your opportunity today?

DAY 13

ESTHER 2 // ESTHER // AWKWARD??

How was Esther awkward? That's a great question! I am so glad you asked! I ask myself the same question all the time about the people I meet who think they are awkward! I say to myself, "You have everything! How can you feel so awkward?". I have come to realize that it does not matter what anyone else thinks. If people see themselves as awkward, or (insert your favorite self-depraving word) then it is a challenge to help them overcome themselves. I find the story of Esther is a great redemptive illustration for just this situation.

Esther was a Jewish orphan girl being raised by her uncle Mordecai, who happened to be a high commander in the King's army. The king got rid of his wife because he feels she betrayed him, and he begins the search for a new wife. Mordecai saw this as an opportunity to put his niece into a better position in life. He believed that she could win the King's heart. Esther on the other hand, was not so sure of this. She saw herself as just a plain orphan girl, how could she compete for the King's heart against the most beautiful woman in the land.

Have you ever felt that way? Like you weren't smart enough, pretty enough, or "whatever" enough. I bet you would be surprised to find out that you are not alone in this feeling. You are not alone! From little kids to grandparents, at one time or another, even the most confident person on the planet has felt this. Like they don't have what it takes to know, or do, or act, or be a certain way. The root of this feeling comes from not fully understanding your identity. Your identity as a child of God, not a child God lets live in His house, but a true son or daughter of the most High King of the land.

The great illustration we read in this story, the story of Esther, is that she had someone around her who believed in her. Often times we don't give credit to the people that are around us who are there cheering us on, believing we can achieve anything. We are so consumed by our own awkwardness that we don't listen to those around us who are asking us to be brave and to step out in faith and believe them, even if we don't believe it yet for ourselves.

We can all be thankful that Esther trusted Mordecai. She believed the words that he said, she stepped out in faith and entered herself in the competition for queen. The great, redemptive part of this story is that she was chosen. The king chose Esther to be his bride. This simple Jewish girl, who didn't think she had what it would take to win the king's heart, and become queen, actually did.

I love that Esther really didn't have anything to lose. If she wasn't chosen as queen, she went back to her life as it always was; but she had everything to gain. How often in life are we paralyzed by the choice to step out, when really what's the worst that could happen? The worst that could happen is you hear the answer no, or you don't succeed. But really have you lost anything? The answer to this question is no. We are being prompted to step out, we fail to understand that we truly have nothing to lose.

What are the areas in life that the Lord is calling you out? Where is He asking you to take a leap of faith and trust that you have what it takes even if you don't think you do? The truth is we all start out this way. We all start out not knowing if we have what it takes, but we take a leap of faith, we start somewhere, and believe just enough to move - and the great thing is, often times that's all it takes! That first step makes you believe that you can take the second, and then the third!

QUESTION // ANSWER

Where do you need to step out in faith today?

Who do you have around you who believes in you?

If you do step out and fail, what is the worst that can happen?

ESTHER 4 // ESTHER // SUCH A TIME
AS THIS

My favorite part of the story of Esther is she was in the
place she was for a particular reason; to set her
people free. She was made for "such a time as this".
How often have you thought to yourself that you are
in the right place at the right time? God is at work all
around us, if we look for where he is at work, often we
find ourselves in the midst of a great moment in
history or another persons life. I don't know if very
many of us really truly understand the moments that
we are in. The old saying goes that hindsight is 20/20
meaning when you look back at a situation you can
see it clearly.

Esther knew she was her people's only hope. She knew
that regardless of how she was feeling she had to find
a way to push through the feelings of fear, anxiety,
and awkwardness to be able to approach the king and
plead for her people.

There will come times in your life where you will feel
awkward about a situation. Like there has to be
another way, but there will come a time where you
truly have to "push through" the feelings of being
awkward, embrace the struggle, and reach out to get
to the resolution that needs to happen.

When Mordecia came to her, she didn't jump up and
down with excitement, and glee. She tried to plead with
him that there would have to be another way. She
couldn't believe that the destiny of her people was laid
on her shoulders. But God gave Esther the strength to

save her people. Esther was brave, and because she stepped out in faith, she became queen. Do you sometimes forget that God is all knowing? He gives us the choice - but He is all knowing. He knew a way was made for the Jewish people when Esther began to follow her uncle to become Queen. And Esther was obedient to the call that was surely in her heart; she had a tugging that God had created her for more than ordinary life. That tugging must have come again when Mordecai came to Esther with the plot that Haman had to destroy the Jewish people. She answered the call and pressed into God. She fasted, prayed and commissioned the Jewish people to fast with her. Esther understood leadership meant risk, we're are all called to be leaders in the faith. There will come times where that call will tug at your heart. Will you be as quick as Esther to answer it?

Understanding her identity was an important part of the confidence Esther had facing the next challenge. Her initial reaction of not thinking she was good enough to become queen was obviously gone. When she was faced with the challenge of going in front of the king when she was not called, she felt certain that if it was God's will then she would be well taken care of. She was bold enough to go to the throne of God and petition the Lord for favor. You also have the right to go before the Lord and petition Him for favor in whatever situation you are facing. The Bible tells us to go boldly before the throne ask, and it shall be given. This is what the Lord desires. He wants to help you, He is seeking relationship with you, to build you up in your faith. You must be brave, seek His face and boldly step out in the destiny that is in your heart. You too, were made for such a time as this!

QUESTION // ANSWER

Is there an area in your life that you need to petition the Lord?

What situations are you facing that remind you of Esther's?

ESTHER 5 // ESTHER // FIRST YOUR IDENTITY, THEN THE TEST COMES

Being awkward is not always a bad thing. Awkward moments are often the times that define us, connect us to others, and build relationship. What happens once you embrace the awkwardness you possess? You know you have met those really confident people who you look at and think to yourself, "How are they so together and I am such a mess?" The reality is, they have embraced who they are! We have seen this through the stories that we have been reading, and Esther's story presents the biggest example of once you understand who you are, that idea will be tested.

Esther embraced her place as queen, and then she was tested with the knowledge that she was her people's only choice. When you begin to acknowledge your Kingdom identity, your identity will be tested. How do you prepare for such a test you ask? Easy, I say! Here is how:

Fill your mind with the Word of God - especially the parts where He is declaring who you are in the Bible. Embrace who you are! I suggest making a list of all the ways that you are unique. Things you like and the things that maybe you don't care so much for. Write this in a place where you can easily look back at it. Write yourself a note that describes why you are special.

Write out your personal declarations. Combine the word of the Lord with your unique qualities and write out your declarations - then use them! When you are having a rough time, remember that you have been made for such a time as this! Surround yourself with people who build you up and encourage you! Find other like-minded people to hang out with. Rid yourself of people who put you down or who don't embrace who you are, who want you to conform to their ideal.

Remember that showing love to people is not the same as being a doormat.

I realize that these four steps are not rocket science, in fact this is probably not the first time you have heard any of these ideas. I challenge you to actually put into action each one of these steps and see the potential that God has for you! Not one of these awkward people in the Bible realized their potential until God declared it.

We are fortunate that God speaks to us today. He has sent the Holy Spirit to be our comforter, and He is here to declare over us how God sees us. We have the Bible, which is the actual Word of God and is a declaration itself of who we are.

Once you embrace who you are, like Esther, you will be able to see clearly, go boldly before the throne of God and make requests of the King. You will be able to live each day to the fullest of its potential, not being plagued by the enemy who is trying to rob you of your destiny and destroy your future.

QUESTION // ANSWER

Take the four ways of embracing who you are and evaluate where you are. Where do you need to grow?

Have you begun to embrace who you are (accept your identity) and felt the challenge of the enemy?

How are you combating his attacks? You must declare the Word of the Lord over your life.

DAY 16

ACTS 9:36-43// DORCAS //TABITHA
#NOTAWKWARDENOUGH

Dorcas is unlike most of the people that we have and will talk about in this book, who truly have some awkwardness surrounding their story... Dorcas does not. In fact there is no actual reason that she would be in this book outside of the fact that her name is Dorcas (a name which is used as an insult in current times). I wanted to include her in this book because, in Biblical times the name Dorcas would not have incited any sort of stigma, but today it would. From the title of todays devotional, Dorcas translated from Hebrew, actually means Tabitha, and the name Tabitha means "a gazelle" – an emblem of beauty.

I want to share about her character even more than the meaning of her name. Sometimes we overlook stories in the Bible, like the story of Dorcas, because her name is unusual. Or maybe it is because in comparison to all the other people that are mentioned in the Bible, she is not mentioned much. Her story is a powerful one and I feel that if the Holy Spirit inspired writing about a woman named Dorcas, we should sit up and take notice.

We know from reading about Dorcas that she was known for her acts of kindness and her charity. The Bible says "which she continually did". This is an important distinction. It speaks to the presentness of her actions. It was not something she had done and it was not some story of the past. At the time of this story, she could have been found at any moment participating in these acts of kindness.

What are you currently known for? What "acts" are you participating in right now? If someone were to write a snippet about you, what would they say? This is one of the most powerful reminders to me to constantly be looking for what God is doing in the moment, how I can partner with Him, and how that ties into the call and future that I have.

Dorcas' story doesn't end with her being mentioned for her good deeds. We know that she fell ill and died. Because of her good deeds we see that many are distraught by her death and send for Peter to come to them. Peter sends everyone out of the room, he prays and speaks to her body and tells her to "arise", and she does.

Two things strike me about this story. One I have already mentioned; how are we known? A question that has come up in my life is: If our church closed the doors would anyone miss us? I think this is a great evaluation of the impact that we are having for Christ, but more importantly, if you die, move, whatever who will miss you? Dorcas had a whole town of widows who not only missed her but warred for her life even in death.

The second thing that strikes me about this story is that she came back to life! That means her work wasn't over. We all have work to do for the Kingdom. It is a matter of unpacking your destiny and setting your hands to do that work. It was clear that Dorcas knew her calling and the Lord was gracious to bring her back to life to complete what she needed to.

QUESTION // ANSWER

What are you doing for the Kingdom right now, that if
you stopped, someone would notice?

What is your "work"? What is your destiny? How are
you partnering with God to complete this?

ACTS 9:36-43// DORCAS // MISSING
YOUR DESTINY

Have you ever been worried that you are missing your "calling"? The story of Dorcas brings us hope, even death cannot stop you from getting to your calling if you are obedient to the word of the Lord. I cannot tell you how many people feel as though they have either missed the calling of the Lord, or are "waiting" to hear from the Lord about their calling.

I bet it frustrated Dorcas to no end when she got sick! She was diligently working in the calling that the Lord had for her. She provided for many widows, many of whom stood by her bed weeping and pleading for her life. Her resurrection, I imagine, was a great stirring for many of the people around her. Imagine that today!

What would happen if you were working hard serving the Lord, you got ill and died – but the Lord resurrected you because your work was not over! How much harder would you work knowing that your job on earth was so important that the Lord sent someone to raise you from the dead?

Understanding your identity and the direction your life is headed is the concern and focus you should have now. You might be thinking that you are too young, or too old, or you missed your mark. But Philippians 1:6 says "being confident of this very thing, that He who has begun a good work in you will complete it until the day of Jesus Christ;" The Lord is faithful to finish working on you and with you till the end of your days or until Christ returns.

We have work to do. Be encouraged! No matter what stage of life you are in, you have work to do for the Kingdom. Habakkuk 2:3 tells us to write down our goals and wait patiently. Things won't happen right away but neither will they be delayed. Dorcas probably didn't know at first the impact she was going to have in her community; she was just being obedient, using her talent and skills as a dressmaker to further the word of the Lord.

Dorcas was a dressmaker – who was brought back to life. I am sure that many people were reached for the glory of the Lord because of this, but I want to point out that she was not some major evangelist, or motivational speaker, or pastor, She was a dressmaker. She had a skill and she put it to good use for the Kingdom of God. What is your skill? Maybe you are in school right now and you are still discovering what your skills are, but I know that you have them. God has given each of us a destiny and the ability to fulfill it. It is our job to start by making the plan and then setting our hands to work, that it may be completed.

Lastly, we need to remember that whatever we ask of the Lord we receive because we keep His commandments (1 John 3:22). As sons and daughters of the King we have at our disposal the fullness of God's goodness. All we have to do is ask. Just like the distressed widows pleaded for the Lord to restore Dorcas' life, God can help you determine and fulfill your calling. If any of you lack, ask of the Lord and He will give it to you!

QUESTION // ANSWER

What are you lacking? Ask the Lord! He is faithful and full of goodness.

Do you have a plan written down? If not, WRITE it. If you do, how are you working towards its completion?

DAY 18

Do you ever feel like following the commandments in the Bible makes you awkward? I am not just talking about the Ten Commandments; I mean the whole thing. Having worked with middle schoolers my entire adult life I have heard how "uncool" the Bible is more times than I care to admit. My response is always the same, the Bible is an outline for your life. It is there to help, guide, and keep you out of harms way.

I get the same response all the time, "My friends are doing it and it's not hurting them," The Bible has a lot to say on this subject, and so do I. Firstly, I would say that more likely than not, if you abstain from doing all the crazy things your friends are doing now, you will thank yourself, and God in fifteen years when you look back at life. I cannot tell you how happy I am that we did not have camera phones, Facebook, Instagram, and YouTube when I was growing up! Sure, we are able to capture all the memories of our lives digitally and relive them over and over and over AND OVER again. Trust me, there will be times in your life that you will wish you didn't have to live them over and over again.

I have had to council more and more students as the years go on about being careful about what they say, do, etc. Not only because it will be captured on the INTERNET for everyone and for always, but also because we are living life without regard to the Bible. We know less about it today than ever before in history. The Bible was not designed to keep you from having fun. It was designed to help you reach your fullest potential and to keep you from a destructive path. The lie of the enemy is that in your youth you don't need to live with purpose, you can live life carefree and without a plan.

The Lord has a plan for your future, but He also has a plan for your present. He has a plan to prosper you NOW. Are you so focused on having fun that you are missing out on these precious years of your youth to study, and practice for future success? Do you know you can start a business, be creative, and be influential now? I have been fascinated lately with successful people. Do you know what one of the things I have realized about successful people is? Many of them started when they were young, with no formal training, but they began at a young age, understanding that they had a destiny beyond their present circumstances.

People with destiny are not only people born with rich parents. EVERYONE is born with a destiny, and your's has been under attack since conception. Maybe you don't know what you want to be when you grow up? You don't even know what you are good at, or what you like to do, but now, when you are young is the time to find those things out. Don't let your friends who are conformed to this world, drag you down and keep you focused on living without purpose during your youth. Be diligent, write out goals each year, and have a plan to achieve them.

QUESTION // ANSWER

What lies are you believing about the Bible being re-strictive instead of equipping?

What do you like to do in your "free time"? How can those interests help you achieve your future plans?

What goals have you set for yourself this year?

If you have not set goals for yourself, set at least three. How are you going to achieve those goals?

Have you ever felt like just because you were young, you couldn't do things? Or because of your age, older people wouldn't listen to you? What an awkward feeling! Instructing older people! Paul, in his letter to Timothy, tells him that he should not let anyone make him feel awkward because of his youth!

What a great bit of encouragement! Paul, one of the greatest disciples of Christ, admonishes (encourages) Timothy to hold fast to the promises that the Lord has given him. Even though he is young, he is a strong leader in the faith. Just because you are young does not disqualify you for leadership. We know from Paul's letter to Timothy that Timothy had been given prophetic words that spoke to the validity of Timothy's leadership and purpose. Also, God saw Timothy's potential, and sent Paul to mentor, encourage, and release him into his destiny.

Do you know that God sees your potential, too! The letters to Timothy are a great place to go to if you are young to begin to unpack your own destiny and future. Feeling awkward because of your age is a normal feeling. It is important to surround yourself with people who not only encourage you, but also who you can learn the word of the Lord from.

Regardless of the potential God sees in you, we are all charged with knowing the scriptures. Paul tells Timothy that there will come a time when false teaching will come. Paul was not just telling this to Timothy; it is recorded in the scriptures for all of us. Just because you are young does not give you the excuse to be ignorant of the word of God and to test the words that are spoken over you or taught to you. You must test them against the word of the Lord to be sure they do not deceive you and send you off your destination.

Has anyone ever prayed for you and told you something about how God sees you? Or maybe God has spoken to you and you believe that you are on a path toward some particular goal; maybe to be a surgeon, a business owner, a missionary, or political leader. You are young and full of the potential of the Lord, but how are you stewarding that? Being wise to your future is something, regardless of age, we must all do. We must have life long goals in order to truly reach our full potential here on earth.

The enemy of your flesh comes to kill your dreams, steal your identity, and destroy destiny. You have weapons that can protect you from this. This is Paul's chief point in writing to Timothy. To encourage his dreams and the prophetic destiny that was spoken over him. Paul wrote to speak identity over Timothy. To remind him who the creator designed him to be and to impart destiny to him. To help him see his future despite the hard times they were facing due to the fact that being a Christian was in large part a crime during this time period. Being a Christian right now might not be a crime, but is sure is unpopular. Being righteous and following the Lord is not going to make you the most popular person. This is the reason Paul was writing to encourage Timothy and you to stay the course. Hold fast to your dreams and know that you have potential!

QUESTION // ANSWER

Do you recognize your potential? If not, has anyone
else? If not, ask the Lord now. Pray this prayer:
"Lord reveal to me how you see me" and quietly wait
for Him to answer. If you hear anything that is not
encouraging or speaking destiny or life it is the enemy.
Rebuke the lie in Jesus' name and ask the Lord to speak
louder so you can hear."

How are you going to steward your potential?

I TIM 1:5-14 // TIMOTHY // DON'T BE ASHAMED OF THE GOSPEL

The gospel? Is the gospel awkward? Well, some people think it is! How often are you sharing what you believe about the Bible? Do you share freely, or is there often a twinge of anxiety attached when what you believe comes up in conversation? First, I want to say you are not alone. You are not a bad person because of this. I am sure the enemy of our flesh would love nothing more than to make you feel like you have somehow missed the mark by not proclaiming your faith from the roof tops every time the opportunity comes up. Stop that thought from entering your mind. Take it captive and rebuke it.

In 2 Timothy 1:8-12, Paul charges Timothy to not be ashamed of the Gospel. Why would Paul have to instruct Timothy, this great disciple of Christ to not be ashamed? Because Paul knew that there would come a time when someone, or something would attempt to make Timothy "ashamed" to call himself a Christian.

Have you ever had a situation come up where you felt "ashamed" to be a Christian? Maybe it happened during history class and your teacher or your friends used the Christian crusade's (over 1000 years ago) to make you feel like being a Christian meant that you were a mass murder. Or maybe something came up on the news about people who call themselves "Christians" treating others poorly. You are not alone. Throughout the Bible and history, Christians have had to fight against the negative image that the enemy tries to paint. It is in those times that you must know the scriptures and what the Word of God says about situations so that you can bring truth into those situations with love. Love is the greatest commandment according to Jesus. First, to love your God with all your heart, your soul, and your mind. Second, to love your neighbor as yourself. It can feel awkward or make you feel ashamed when you see others acting out of judgment rather than love. You are tasked with coming with the opposite spirit; we are called to love the sinner and hate the sin. Christ was known for hanging out with and being around sinners. Why? He said that doctors see patients so that they might be healed and He comes as the healer to heal the broken hearted. As ambassadors of Christ it is our job to be healers to the broken hearted.

I am not saying that you should put yourself in dangerous situations just to share the gospel, but I am saying that you should ask the Lord each day to see where He is at work in the Kingdom and where you are to partner. Do not become ashamed of the gospel because there are those out there that are distorting the truth for their own gain. Know the Word of the Lord and seek His desires that you may express the love of the Father everywhere you go.

QUESTION // ANSWER

Are there times when you feel ashamed of the Gospel?

How can you partner with the Lord to further the Kingdom?

ROM 12:3-8 // AS ONE // NO MATTER HOW AWKWARD YOU FEEL!

In Romans 12:3-8 Paul talks about our something to contribute as part of the body of Christ. Each of us is given a different function in the body. If we feel awkward or out of place, how can we serve our purpose in the body of Christ? You are unique. YOU ARE! No one has the exact talents, creativity, and position in the body of Christ. You were created uniquely to be who you are for a purpose. The enemy of your flesh wants you to feel awkward and out of place when you are in the body of Christ so that he can hide your destiny. He projects his own discomfort onto you so that you might not reach your full potential in the Kingdom.

Right now is the best time for you to begin to understand what your gifts, calling, identity, and destiny are. No matter what stage of life you are in, the best time to start is NOW. Too long we have been distracted as Christians from our full potential. We need to get back to the forefront in society. If you look at history you will see countless examples of Christians, followers of the Gospel, were the foremost thinkers in the universe. Why do you think that is?

When God created man He said, "Let us make man in Our image." The creator of the universe created you to be unique and specially qualified to be creative, imaginative, and to reach further into the future than non-believers. You have the creator of all Heaven and all earth at your disposal ready to unlock the secrets of the universe to you!

Despite what critics may say, if we look back at some of the most famous paintings and scientific discoveries in history; they were discovered by Christians OR Jews! Even in recent history, The Lord of the Rings and The Hobbit Trilogy. These are stories adapted from J. R. R. Tolkien, a well known Christian author. Same with the Chronicles of Narnia movies that Disney is releasing. C.S. Lewis is not only a well known Christian author, he was influenced by J.R.R Tolkien, and has influenced much of modern literacy!

You are made to be an influencer. You are not called to work in the shadows of the world. You are called to cast your light in the world. We are made to discover cures for disease and be the most influential political leaders of our time. You are called to be business owners and creatively provide jobs and finances to further the Kingdom. You are called to be world changers and nation shakers!

CAUTION: Do not be envious of the gifts given to others. Do not allow bitterness to creep in and distract you from the call that God has on your life. In Romans 12:6 it says that, "having gifts that differ according to the grace given to us, let us use them...". To each of us is given in accordance with our character and destiny. Do not belittle the gift, or the desires of your heart. If you desire to be a stay at home mom and raise your children, be the best stay at home mom you can be! Do not allow the enemy to make you doubt the gifts and the calling that is on your life. Not everyone is called to be the President of the United States, but some are called and never answer because they are too busy looking at the callings on other people's lives! Always remember, God is here to work things together for our good.

QUESTION // ANSWER

What are the desires of your heart?
(Sketch a picture of it no matter what it looks like)
What gifts has God equipped you with?

How can you use those gifts in the world to further the
Kingdom?

DAY 22

Many of us have heard the verse about God not giving us a spirit of fear, but how is fear making you feel awkward? The feeling of awkwardness has its roots in fear. Paul tells Timothy that the Lord has not given him a spirit of fear but of power, and of love, and of a sound mind. Paul understands that with Timothy being a young man, with great pressure to share the gospel, it is likely a spirit of fear will come to him. Paul is reminding him that fear does not come from the Lord. Your heavenly Father has equipped you to handle your destiny with love and a sound mind.

If we go back a couple of verses, Paul is reminding Timothy to stir up the gifts that Paul imparted to him through the laying on of hands. Basically, Paul is re-minding Timothy that both God, and God through Paul, have equipped Timothy to handle the situations that he will come against. There is no reason that a spirit of fear or awkwardness needs to come in and take hold of the situation, thus preventing you from fulfilling your destiny and calling.

In Romans 12:2, Paul writes that we are not to be conformed to this world, but that we are to be transformed and to take captive our thoughts for the renewing of our minds. God has equipped you with the ability to take captive the feelings of awkwardness and the feelings of fear, submit them to God, and have Him renew your mind. How do you renew your mind?

Your mind is renewed through the teachings of the Bible; through studying the Word. Get around people that know the word and can help you understand it. Submitting your thoughts to the Holy Spirit will also help you to take hold of the spirit of fear and conquer it. We cannot ignore our feelings. If we are feeling fear or awkwardness we need to figure out that feeling and ask the Lord to set us free from oppression. The Lord is faithful to answer.

Timothy had Paul, but at the time Paul was writing to him, he was in jail. Timothy could have easily decided that the risk was too great and that he didn't want the same destiny that Paul had for himself. Paul calls him out and says do not fear, for the Lord is with you and you have what you need. Paul tells him later that the cost is worth it all. The cost of the gospel is worth your life.

There will be times throughout your life, you may be faced with them right now, that a spirit of fear is tormenting you. Know that you do not have to submit to that fear. The Lord has not given it to you. That spirit of fear is from the enemy of your flesh and you have been given all authority in Christ to rebuke it, in His name. The answer will remain the same; renew your mind by studying the word. Identify what the Bible says about your identity, and the character of God, so that when the enemy comes to kill, steal and destroy – you are armed with the full armor of God and ready to battle for the destiny that God has called you to!

QUESTION // ANSWER

Are there areas of your life where you are living with fear? Find two or three Bible verses that speak the opposite of that.

How are you renewing your mind daily?

There are times in the lives of even the best of the best when we have felt awkwardness. At some point in all of our journeys we are faced with a choice to quit and give up, or embrace that awkward feeling, the fear, and take courage and step out in faith. Many "heroes" of the Bible were this same way. They could have quit and gone home because the adversary they faced was too great in their eyes.

The story of Elijah and the 300 prophets of Baal is one of the stories that comes to mind when I think about being faced with a difficult choice. Not because of the victory that Elijah had, but because of the challenge that he faced right after that victory. Have you ever felt like you were on the right path, following after the Lord, having great victory, and then when it was over something bad happened?

I imagine that is how Elijah felt. There he was doing all this good for the Lord, defying the prophets of Baal, then the wife of the king threatens his life. Elijah had JUST called fire from heaven to devour 300 men – and one woman threatens him and sends him into the wilderness for 40 days (If that's not awkward I don't know what is)!

Elijah is not alone in this feeling though. I have heard countless people declare over their lives that "just as soon as something goes right – everything else goes wrong" or "every time something good happens - something bad happens". Have you ever felt this way? I don't want to say this is common, but it is not unheard of. We even have this story to encourage us. Later in the chapter God visits Elijah and gives him great direction, and sees him through this discouraging time. The Lord sends an angel to supernaturally sustain Elijah in the wilderness.

GOD is FAITHFUL! Don't believe the lie of the enemy, that just because something is going wrong, "everything" is going wrong. The Lord is here to guide you through the wilderness and to supernaturally sustain you when you need it. Don't give into the fear that as soon as something good happens, something bad will accompany it. Just as God sustained Elijah and protected him from Jezebel, so can God sustain you and protect you from the enemy.

QUESTION // ANSWER

Be encouraged that when something good is happening, the Lord is at work. He is working on calling forth your destiny, your identity, and your purpose in the Kingdom.

Is there an area of you life where you are waiting for something bad to happen?

DAY 24

1 SAM 16:1-13 // DAVID // JUST A SHEPHERD

I am sure you are thinking that there is nothing awkward about David. He was one of the greatest kings in all of history, right? I agree. I am not writing about David to talk about how awkward he was, but rather, how awkward he was perceived to be, even in his own family.

David was uniquely confident in the Lord, and who he, himeself was. This is evident in the stories we read about him as a young shepherd boy. When the spirit of the Lord came upon David, he was confident and sure that the Lord was with him. But just because he was confident and sure, didn't mean that everyone around him was. Don't get me wrong, after David defeated Goliath there was no doubt for the people that God was with him, but David was still the youngest son, and still young in age and stature. People looked down on him and even Goliath made fun of the king for sending a "boy to do a mans job".

I pray every day that I would have a heart like David's. It is said that the Lord was pleased with him because he was a man after His own heart. David desired to fulfill the desires of God's heart. How awesome! But like David, maybe you have experienced your own self-confidence being mocked in the face of a challenge. Has this happened to you? Have you ever felt so sure that something was going to go your way, only to have others look down their noses at you?

David didn't care. He proclaimed just as the Lord had saved him from the lion and the bear that had come to attack his sheep, the Lord would deliver him from Goliath.

Others will look down on you. You are not called to be set apart in order for everyone to accept everything you say and do. This is the great lesson we learn from David - that sometimes others think we are awkward, but we are not! The Lord has set you apart, and as you walk boldly through the trials that are set before you with confidence in the Lord, God will be with you, just as He was with David.

David was confident in who and whose He was. He knew that he was the anointed one. He knew that the Lord had set him apart and he allowed this knowledge to build up his character and his self-confidence. Sure, he might have even seemed stupidly arrogant walking up to a giant, but because David was sure of the destiny on his life and the identity that God had given him, he was confident in the plans of the Lord.

You need to build your confidence in the Lord, and the first step to doing that is understanding your identity and your place in the Kingdom of God. You were not put on this earth to be conformed to its ways, you have been set apart. Each day we have focused on a great hero or concept from the Bible that can teach you your identity, but like David you must increase your knowledge and understanding if you want to defeat the giants the Lord has called you too. We all have a purpose and a destiny on this earth, and no, the Lord does not need us, but He wants us! He wants us to embrace who we are, and like David, walk up to the giant and already see it defeated before we cast the first stone!

QUESTION // ANSWER

How would you rate your self-confidence on a scale of
1-10?

What is your understanding of your identity? And how
should that increase how you see yourself?

No matter where you land in the birth order, if you are first, last, middle, or an only child, there are certain expectations that come with that place in the birth order. Not only does your family put expectations on you, society does as well. How many times have you heard "oh you must be the baby of the family" or "wow, she is an only child for sure". All these statements assume certain attributes about a person's birth order. Does your birth order make you awkward, NO, but it can incite certain feelings of responsibility.

I am sure that David's brother's reaction to him being anointed as the next king was not all claps and cheers. We have an expectation that the youngest typically does not get to be king, it is usually the eldest. First borns, as they are often referred to, get all the privilege. They are often known for their leadership quality. In many cultures throughout history first-borns obtained all the birthrights whereas the younger had to go out into the world and make a way for themselves.

David was chosen as the last born and astonished even Samuel. When Samuel was sent to anoint the next king from Jesse's household and the brothers were lined up, he stepped forward and went down the line to find the one that the Lord would point out. He started from the oldest and worked his way down in order of birth. My point in this is not to say that one position is better than the other, but rather that all positions of birth and rank in God's eyes can be a privilege. God is not concerned with where you were in the order of your family; He is concerned with your heart.

Did David get flack for this? I am sure he did. We know that when David went to the battlefield to deliver sandwiches his brothers mocked him, but David was so confident in who he was he did not worry about them. We need to follow after David in this. When the Lord has given us a task and asked us to fulfill a duty we need to be sure that we are faithful and confident like David. We need to be sure of our calling. From the moment that David was anointed the Spirit of the Lord was with him, and David knew that he could do anything the Lord asked of him.

The great thing about now, in contrast to when David was anointed, is... When Christ died on the cross, was resurrected, and went to heaven, He sent the Holy Spirit to which we all have equal access. We can partner with the Lord every day. In David's time the Holy Spirit only rested with prophets and kings, but because Christ has restored us to relationship with God as joint-heirs to the throne, we are all able to have the same confidence David did to ignore the taunting of his brothers and fight the giants that we face.

David didn't let his brother's insecurity project awkwardness or doubt onto him. He knew he was anointed and God was with him. He had a destiny and a calling that no one could take away from him but the Lord.

QUESTION // ANSWER

What Giants are you facing that you need the Holy Spirit to strengthen your resolve to fight?

Do others look down on you and try to project their awkwardness onto you?

JOEL 2:18-27 // MISTAKES VS. DESTINY

Regardless of where you are at in life, you have likely made a mistake. Maybe you thought that the mistake you made disqualified you for your destiny. Often when we do finally realize our mistake(s), they make us feel awkward or unable to come before the Lord and ask for forgiveness and ultimately see our destiny restored. Don't worry you are not alone! Throughout the Old Testament the people of Israel were constantly falling away from the Lord and He had to send prophets to help point them to their future and calling.

The book of Joel, which speaks prophetically about things to come, also says in verse 25 that the Lord will restore to you the years that the locust has stolen. We can take this word and lay hold of this testimony in our times of missing the mark as well. This verse tells us that it is within the power of the Lord to restore to us the things that have been missed or taken from us; things that we should have had, that were in line with our own calling.

This is not a verse that is advocating for you to do whatever you want and rely on God's grace to give you everything you need free and clear from the hard labor it takes to produce, but it is saying that He can multiply the time and efforts of your hands.

Perhaps you are at a stage where your learning should be further along than it is, but because you wasted time you missed out. Or perhaps you are behind due to unforeseen circumstances. Being behind does not have to be the answer. Fulfilling your destiny is always the answer. The Lord is faithful to restore the things that have been taken away from you. He is also faithful to restore relationships and callings. Just because there have been situations that have prevented you in the past, those do not have to be defining moments.

I encourage you to take this passage of scripture and lay hold of it for your life. If you have dreams and goals you thought were dead, make this your declaration. Write out those goals and dreams and ask the Lord to guide your steps and help you determine where to begin. The Bible says that He who began a good work is faithful to complete it. That is true for your life, too!

Don't let your mistakes or misguided turns define your life. Be quick to repent and even quicker to obey the word of the Lord. The more you listen and obey the faster and easier it will become to partner with the Lord. Do not allow your old life of disobedience or mis-guidance to define your future.

QUESTION // ANSWER

What dreams and aspirations did you think were dead?

How can you partner with the Lord to see those
dreams fulfilled?

1 SAM 18 // DAVID // IN THE KING'S HOUSE

The story of David prior to becoming a king gives us insight on what it means to have others underestimate or be threatened by your potential. David's brothers mocked him for thinking he could defeat Goliath, but King Saul brought David into the castle. King Saul needed something that only David had. Your talents and abilities will take you places that no one else can get to.

Each of us is created with a different set of talents and a different calling. If David's talents and skills ended where his brother's or father's did, he would have remained a shepherd; but he was destined to be a king. When Saul brought David into his trust, David found favor with him.

The Lord desires to grant you favor. He desires to help you in every situation that you are in to find your purpose and be successful. Do you think that once David was anointed king, that he was "ready" to be king? No! The Lord had to take David through a refining process; a process in which his character and resolve was both formed and tested.

When Saul discovered that David was God's anointed one, he grew jealous of him. He even tried to get his own son, David's best friend, on his side. When people see you stepping into your destiny and see you blessed with the favor of the Lord in your circumstances, it can make them envious and make them do things that could cause you harm. Saul would throw spears at David.

In your life, when you begin to step out into your dreams there may be those around you who are un-happy with the LACK of faith that they have had, and they may say mean things, or do mean things to you. Do not let this distract you.

Do what David did. He dodged the spears, but re-mained true to his duty. Even in the midst of Saul throwing spears at David, he remained honoring to not only the authority of Saul, the King of Israel, but also to the faith that he held onto regarding his own destiny.

It is important to have your goals written somewhere you can always look to them to have your faith built up. You will start small but as your experience progress-es, so will the victories and stories you will have to be thankful for. David didn't start with Goliath, he started protecting his sheep, but soon was the man who killed 10,000 Philistines. David had much to be proud of and thankful for.

Remember also that as your friends begin to see their dreams and destiny become a reality not to allow bitterness or offense to creep in while you work to fulfill your dreams. We see this with Saul's son Jonathan. He did not allow for the success and the destiny of David to cause him pain, he submitted to the will of the Lord that even though he would be the heir to the throne because of his birth, God chose someone else and Jonathan was faithful to support David even when his father did not.

QUESTION // ANSWER

Are you keeping honor intact with your peers and your leaders?

Are you respecting and cheering others on in their quest for destiny?

DAY 28

JUDGES 7 // GIDEON // LEADER OF MANY

To most people Gideon is known as the least of the least, whom God called a mighty man of valor. Gideon was also known as the leader of the valiant three hundred. As we have seen throughout our study on awkward people of the Bible, God has repeatedly taken people who either did not understand their value, or who others had grossly under estimated. We opened with a story of Gideon and now we will look at what kind of a leader he really was.

Do you ever doubt that people are following you? Maybe, like Gideon, you see yourself as the least of the least. That no one would really be following you. The fact of the matter is that if we are Christians we are all called to be leaders; and not just leaders, but leaders of leaders. We are commissioned by Jesus to go and make disciples of all nations. ALL of us are charged to go and make disciples and teach those disciples how to make disciples and so on.

God used a few men in Gideon's story to show His miraculous delivery of the Midianites into His hands, but God still wanted Gideon to be the leader. God chose Gideon because He saw the heart of the man. He knew that He could count on him. He also knew that Gideon would follow and allow the Lord to be victorious. God used 300 men to defeat a multitude. He did it through the leadership and guidance of one man; one man who was submitted to the leadership of his Heavenly Father.

As we reach out, seek our destiny and get into battles that seem too large for us to handle, it does not negate our need to be a leader. Being a leader means submitting to the leadership of your leader, God. The Lord will partner with you for His glory to bring you into the fullness of your destiny. God knew Gideon's heart was noble. He trusted Gideon to follow when he would need to follow.

This is what the Lord is asking of us. He has given us the freedom to choose to partner with Him, and as do He is faithful to fulfill the desires of our heart. Your Heavenly Father wants what is best for you. He does not make plans that would make you unhappy, or plans that would ultimately cause you to suffer. We may not always have sunshine and roses to deal with, but God is faithful to complete the good works He has in store for us.

Just like Gideon, God is calling you to be a mighty woman/man of valor. He is equipping you to defeat untold numbers of adversaries with the resources He has given you. He wants us to be dependent on Him so that we can learn and grow in Him. The more we learn, the better we can follow, and the better we will lead also. There are times in every leader's life where you are called to both serve and lead. It is your duty to serve the people you lead as well as the people you follow. The better equipped you are to follow, the better equipped you are to lead.

Don't let anyone make you feel like you are too awkward, or small, or young, to accomplish the goals that the Lord has set before you. He has called you - NOW answer the call!

QUESTION // ANSWER

Are there areas you feel like the Lord is asking too
much of you?

Who are you following? Why? (DRAW A DIAGRAM)
Who is following you?

2 SAM 17 & 18// DAVID AND SONS // WHO'S AWKWARD NOW?

King David was known as having a heart after God's heart. He was known for being confident in the Lord. When he had many sons and was of old age, Absalom attempted to turn the Kingdom against David. David, still being confident in who the Lord had made him to be ran and hid from his son. David ordered his men to not kill his son.

How crazy is that? It seems a little cowardly, maybe even a little awkward. The king is hiding from his son who is trying to kill him, and the king tells his men to not kill his son!? Why!? Because David LOVED his son. There is much to learn from this story. First, let's recap.

David was called as a young man to be a king. He was the youngest in his family. Then, still as a young boy he found favor with King Saul. He killed a Philistine giant named Goliath. THEN the king found out that David was God's anointed to take over the Kingdom and then he became threatened by David, and tried for many years to kill him. David was still confident in who he was. When Saul died David honored him. He ascended the throne and served the country well. Sure, he had a lapse in judgment, but he repented and his heart remained in alignment with God's. It is no wonder that in his old age, when his son tried to take over the Kingdom, David let the Lord handle the situation how He would.

Can you imagine being that confident in who you are, and whose you are? God was so pleased with David that He made sure that the Messiah would come out of his lineage. The savior of the whole world would come from King David – a man after God's own heart. Think of the promises of God! What are the promises that God has made to you? Maybe He hasn't made any yet that you know of. The Bible is full of God's promises to us. That is the great thing about studying the Word. God hides treasures for us in it. The Psalms are a great place to start looking for treasures from Lord. They are written in large part by David, and are there for us today to have full access to the same promises.

The sad part of the story is that Absalom ends up being killed in the woods by accident while chasing after his father. David is deeply wounded by this. God also mourns over his lost sons and daughters, too. Like King David, God is not out to make sure He is right and we are wrong. When we get off target He tries to bring us back. I am sure you have seen people stop serving the Lord in your lifetime. Maybe you have even seen the Lord reach out to them and try to bring them back. Like the story of the good shepherd, leaving the ninety-nine in search for the lost one, the Lord is faithful to seek after His lost sheep. Who do you know that would be considered a lost sheep? Do you pray that they would find their way back to the Lord?

QUESTION // ANSWER

Do you have promises that you are waiting to see fulfilled by the Lord?

Who are the lost sheep the Lord has placed on your
heart? If you don't have any that come to mind, ask
Him and He will bring them to you.

DAY 30

After 29 days of looking at awkward people from the Bible, people that most would consider great heroes of the faith, can you see your calling and future lined in the greatness of these heroes? Do you still feel like you are not good enough, strong enough, or pretty or handsome enough?

Are you an eloquent speaker like Moses?
Are you strong and mighty like Gideon?
Are you wholesome and pure like Gomer?
Have you finished all you set your hands to like Dorcas?
Maybe you are old and wise like Timothy?
Perhaps you are confident like Peter was?
Does everyone around you have faith in you, just like David's family?
Maybe you know you are a beautiful queen like Esther?

Wait a minute... no one thought that Moses had what it took to lead the people of Israel out of captivity, except God. Not even Gideon thought he was strong and mighty, except God. Gomer wasn't wholesome and pure, but God loved her anyway. Dorcas had much work to do still on earth and yet she died, but God raised her. Paul encouraged Timothy that even though he was young he needed to have faith and expect God! Peter was a coward and denied Jesus but still went on to be a forerunner for the Christian faith. David was the youngest in his family, and even as God's anointed suffered great persecution. Esther didn't know that she was destined to be queen, but God did.

No matter what you think makes you awkward, no matter if some or none of the stories helped you see beyond your awkwardness, you need to learn to expect God and allow Him to work in all situations that would seem hopeless.

When we can allow the Holy Spirit to come into our lives to teach us to expect the Lord to show up, to expect Him to be for us and not against us, then we can have a hope and a future that is built on the goodness of God. He is the good shepherd; He has plans to prosper you and not to harm you!

Take this time in your life and embrace the awkwardness that makes you unique and makes you a son or a daughter of the most high King! Start to live out of your destiny and your identity in Christ, instead of the despair and the false identity this world would have you believe! You have been born for such a time as this! You are not an accident! God knew you from the time He formed you in the womb! Embrace Him and embrace who He made you to be!

FORGIVENESS PRAYER
By Neil T. Anderson // THE BONDAGE BREAKER
© Dec 15, 2006 pg. 225

Pray the following:

God, I am choosing to forgive (?)
for (what they did/didn't do or made you feel)
because i felt (...)
I choose not to hold onto my anger and/or frustration
and/or hurt. I thank you that you set me free from
those feelings Lord. I let go of my right to seek revenge
and ask you to heal my damaged emotions. I pray a
blessing over those who hurt me in Jesus name.

Amen

OTHER TITLES AND MATERIALS COMING SOON!

AWKWARD PEOPLE OF THE BIBLE 2

AWKWARD BIBLE STUDY

AWKWARD SUNDAY MORNINGS
FINDING YOUR IDENTITY AND RELEASING YOUR DREAMS

DAUGHTER OF THE SHEPHERD, HEIR TO THE THRONE

Made in the USA
Middletown, DE
05 July 2015